THIS IS ME!

MY FAVOURITE THINGS

Edited By Jenni Harrison

First published in Great Britain in 2022 by:

YoungWriters®
Est. 1991

Young Writers
Remus House
Coltsfoot Drive
Peterborough
PE2 9BF
Telephone: 01733 890066
Website: www.youngwriters.co.uk

All Rights Reserved
Book Design by Ashley Janson
© Copyright Contributors 2021
Softback ISBN 978-1-80015-814-6

Printed and bound in the UK by BookPrintingUK
Website: www.bookprintinguk.com
YB0496L

FOREWORD

For Young Writers' latest competition This Is Me, we asked primary school pupils to look inside themselves, to think about what makes them unique, and then write a poem about it! They rose to the challenge magnificently and the result is this fantastic collection of poems in a variety of poetic styles.

Here at Young Writers our aim is to encourage creativity in children and to inspire a love of the written word, so it's great to get such an amazing response, with some absolutely fantastic poems. It's important for children to focus on and celebrate themselves and this competition allowed them to write freely and honestly, celebrating what makes them great, expressing their hopes and fears, or simply writing about their favourite things. This Is Me gave them the power of words. The result is a collection of inspirational and moving poems that also showcase their creativity and writing ability.

I'd like to congratulate all the young poets in this anthology, I hope this inspires them to continue with their creative writing.

CONTENTS

Crazies Hill CE Primary School, Wargrave

George Wetherell (7)	1
Jemima Stone (8)	2
Bo Fyffe (9)	3
Roberta Pope (9)	4
Felix Reynolds-Kasprzyk (8)	5
Ophelia Wood (7)	6
Evie Clark (7)	7
Finnley James (8)	8
Othello Forbes (7)	9
Thomas Elford (7)	10
Milo Sharp (7)	11
Albert Sutherland (7)	12
Sophia Stavrou (8)	13
Ella Peters (9)	14
Ben Webster (8)	15
Isla-Jean Preece (9)	16
Jason Bennett (8)	17
Peter Sly (7)	18
Mario Tong (8)	19

East Peckham Primary School, East Peckham

Tariq Tandjiora (10)	20
Esther Brown (10)	21
Evie Cooper (10)	22
Emily Bastable (10)	24
Thomas Fox (11)	26
Thomas Woodhams (10)	27
Abigail Hearn (10)	28
Abel Thomas (10)	29
George Ridley (10)	30
Archie Wilson (10)	31

Poppy Jones (10)	32
Sophie Webb (11)	33
Lena Geehan (11)	34
Ethan Coleman (10)	35

Eccleston St Mary's CE Primary School, Eccleston

Arthur R (10)	36
Freya W (10)	38
Grace R (10)	39
Lillia Marsden (10)	40
Holly McLaughlin (10)	41
Mia Watson (10)	42
Matthew C (10)	43
Mia Dodoo (10)	44
Alex K (10)	45
Lucas B (10)	46
Ava Juliette Craghill (10)	47
Kate Jackson (10)	48

Edward Wilson Primary School, Westminster

Laila Youssef (11)	49
Zubaydah Aktar (10)	50
Yousif Qazizada (10)	51
Hassan Ali (10)	52
Emily Kaboli (10)	53

Falconbrook Primary School, Battersea

Sabrina Khan (8)	54
Ishrah Azgaoc (8)	55
Sofia Porto (8)	56

Iman Asif (8)   57

Hazelbury Primary School, Edmonton

Chloe Ramsay (10)	58
Nicholas Lambrou (11)	60
Leo Mensah (10)	62
Cairo Roberts-Dabner (10)	64
Mumtaz Mohamed (11)	65
Mikayla Morgan (11)	66
Jayden Moore (10)	67
Tiana K N Kironde (10)	68
Nafisa Mohamed (10)	69
Kavya Matadar (10)	70
Raul Poara (10)	71
Lola Warne (10)	72
Omer Muhammed Sanci (11)	73

King Edward Primary School, North Shields

Ella Basherville (10)	74
Juliette Herzberg (11)	76
Billie Pickles (10)	78
Florence Chambers (10)	79
Sebastian Knowles (11)	80
Matilda Ironside (10)	81
Katie Dixon (10)	82
Beau Heslop (10)	83
Connie Culyer (10)	84
Joshua Burgon (10)	86
Asa Mather (11)	87
Hamzah Islam (10)	88
Alexandra Dunn (10)	89
Archie Duckworth (10)	90
Liam Grant (11)	91
Jack Cullerton-White	92
Lucas Armstrong (10)	93
Maisie Heskett (10)	94
Alfie Taylor (10)	95
Sara Turnbull (10)	96
Zach Cottingham (11)	97
Olivia Gregg (10)	98

Liam Nicholson (11)	99
Joshua Rutherford (11)	100
Amy Dillon (10)	101
Jake Beavers (10)	102
Archie Brown (11)	103
Polly Binks (10)	104
Faith Callaghan (10)	105
Luisa Gray (11)	106

Kingswood Parks Primary School, Kingswood

Isaac Franks (8)	107
Naomi Skorczewski (9)	108
Amelia W (10)	109
Gracie C (8)	110
Vanesa C (8)	111
Edee Frankie Silvester (8)	112
Ivy B (8)	113
Grace Gill Howard (7)	114
Ella McGrath (9)	115
Maria Jackson (7)	116

Larks Hill J&I School, Pontefract

Jake Thompson (9)	117
Mia Jocek (8)	118
Olivia Crompton (8)	119

Little Heaton CE Primary School, Rhodes

Darcy M (7)	120
Poppy Collins (7)	121
T'mia Uff (8)	122
Kaggwa Mawanda (7)	123
Lilia Rogers (7)	124
Renee Rogers (7)	125
Harper Smith (8)	126
Annabelle Garrod (8)	127
Leo Johnson (7)	128
Cole Moore (8)	129
Kylan Roberts-Hall (7)	130
Layla King (7)	131

Jonah Holdsworth (7)	132
Louis Trylski (7)	133
Reggie Boyd (7)	134
Ernests Dreimanis (7)	135
Millie Smith (8)	136
Leighton Cleary (7)	137
Emmie Irving (7)	138
Lilly Garrity (8)	139

Machanhill Primary School, Machanhill

Orla Downs (10)	140
Emily Fernon (10)	142
Lexi Guy (10)	143
William Boyd (10)	144
Aimee Newlands (9)	145
Caius Ian Mullen (10)	146
Naomi Taylor (10)	147
Sam Bishop (10)	148
CJ Hamilton (10)	149
Dylan Hunter (10)	150
Kirsten Ferguson Walker (10)	151
Coll Watson (9)	152
Scarlett Semple (9)	153
Philip Spence (10)	154
Kayla Rundell (10)	155

Smith's Wood Primary Academy, Smith's Wood

Macorley Jevons (11)	156
Gracie-Leigh Wood (10)	157
Demi-Leigh Gouldingay (8)	158
Mahrosh Fatima (7)	159
Olly Herbert (8)	160
Ava Hill (8)	161
Hazel Lang-Amug (7)	162
Lilly-Rose Manders (7)	163
Jaiden-Epie Nnoko (8)	164
Sophie Mullins (8)	165
Summer Rose (7)	166
Harrison Turner (8)	167
Ethan Watkins (7)	168

Tayah Stephens (8)	169
Aarya Patel (7)	170
Jack Phillips (8)	171
Poppy Andrews (7)	172
Seanna Tipper (10)	173
Isabelle Hickin (7)	174
Isabella Walton (7)	175
Flynn Hickling (7)	176
Autumn Rose (7)	177
Evanna Howell-Roberts (7)	178
Millie Duffen (7)	179
Riley Summers (7)	180
Bradley Morris (8)	181
Kacie-Leigh Snook (7)	182
Amelia Bunford (7)	183
Nouria Mata (10)	184
Cialan Nolan (7)	185
Lucy Roberts (7)	186
Vinny Harper (7)	187
Louie Simmonds (7)	188
Riley Stanley (8)	189
Finley Andrews (7)	190

St Stephen's CE Primary School, Westminster

Beverly Garia (7)	191
Sumaya Nur (7)	192

The Kibworth School, Kibworth Beauchamp

Isabel Rhodes (11)	193
Alaina Scott (11)	194
Orla Kempster (11)	196
Izzy Moore (11)	198
Noah Purves (11)	199
Ennio Pizzorno (11)	200
Milli Coulter-Crozier (11)	201
Elliot Hartley (11)	202
Sophie Boulter (11)	203
Imogen (11)	204
Charlie Robinson (12)	205

The Literacy House International, Tintagel

Tahir Eralp Guzel (11)   206

Thorpedene Primary School, Shoeburyness

Theo Oryem (7)   208

THE POEMS

This Is Me

T iger lover
H ates cheese a lot more than tuna
I like swimming with my family
S and is annoying as it goes in your eyes

I like elephants as they are my favourite animal
S inging is not my style

M onkeys are cheeky like me
E lephants have never forgotten anything in their life!

George Wetherell (7)
Crazies Hill CE Primary School, Wargrave

This Is Me

T asty pizza in my tummy
H orse riding is my favourite hobby
I love rollerblading but I like running too
S chool is the best

I snore at night and daydream in the day
S now is my favourite weather

M y birthday is in December
E aster is my favourite celebration.

Jemima Stone (8)
Crazies Hill CE Primary School, Wargrave

This Is Me
A kennings poem

I am a...
Footballer
Hip hop dancer
Baker
Harry Potter fan
Sweet eater
Reptile lover
Sewing lover
Descendants lover
Music lover
Break dancer
Food lover
Great drawer
Book reader
Strictly watcher
Pizza lover
Baby sitter
Big sister
Last but not least
A skateboarder.

Bo Fyffe (9)
Crazies Hill CE Primary School, Wargrave

This Is Me
A kennings poem

I am a...
Puppy lover
Fashion designer
Book reader
Video gamer
Bug fleer
Football player
Art maker
Constant chatter
BFF haver
Chocolate eater
Purple liker
Pink hater
Music listener
Disney watcher
Piano player
And finally...
A Harry Potter lover.

Roberta Pope (9)
Crazies Hill CE Primary School, Wargrave

This Is Me

T rees are my favourite thing to draw
H ot dogs are my favourite food
I am a great football player
S nakes are my favourite animal

I love to ride my bike
S inging is my worst talent

M y dogs are very playful
E ating steak is delicious.

Felix Reynolds-Kasprzyk (8)
Crazies Hill CE Primary School, Wargrave

This Is Me

T V lover
H umming every day makes all my worries go away
I gloos are my favourite type of house
S queeze hugger

I maginary fighter
S nakes are one of my favourite animals

M y heart is full of love and kindness
E mu lover.

Ophelia Wood (7)
Crazies Hill CE Primary School, Wargrave

This Is Me

T ries lots of dance moves
H as lots of Lego
I s very good at skateboarding
S tares at the TV

I s definitely in love with dogs
S inging Harvey songs all the time

M y eyes are sparkling blue
E ating burgers a lot.

Evie Clark (7)
Crazies Hill CE Primary School, Wargrave

This Is Me

T all as a two-year-old
H as amazing football skills
I like animals
S wimming in the water, my dad's my hero

I like to help people
S and I like to play in

M usic gets me going
E lephants, I like, are big.

Finnley James (8)
Crazies Hill CE Primary School, Wargrave

This Is Me

T errible Minecraft player
H ot chocolate lover
I nventing person
S weet eater

I ncredible Lego builder
S illy pizza demolisher

M agical dragon communicator
E xcellent birthday person.

Othello Forbes (7)
Crazies Hill CE Primary School, Wargrave

This Is Me

T o do a lot of Lego
H ugging Miss Cooper
I love cheetahs
S easide and making sandcastles

I magine being in Star Wars
S haring my snacks

M e doing dressing up
E ating chocolate.

Thomas Elford (7)
Crazies Hill CE Primary School, Wargrave

This Is Me

A kennings poem

Football lover
Animal lover
Shark lover
Friends keeper
Fun keeper
Technology designer
Happy lover
Swimming lover
TV watcher
Blue painter
Lego lover
Maths solver
Fast runner
Eager reader
Peaceful person.

Milo Sharp (7)
Crazies Hill CE Primary School, Wargrave

This Is Me
A kennings poem

I am a...
Mario Kart player
Roast chicken eater
Big brother
Lego builder
Music listener
Star Wars watcher
Christmas lover
Football player
Rapid runner
Creative drawer
And finally...
A good helper!

Albert Sutherland (7)
Crazies Hill CE Primary School, Wargrave

This Is Me
A kennings poem

I am a...
Good dressmaker
Great baker
Dog lover
Harry Potter watcher
Great footballer
I have one brother
Fast reader
Good listener
Purple liker
Speedy runner
And finally...
Movie lover.

Sophia Stavrou (8)
Crazies Hill CE Primary School, Wargrave

This Is Me

A kennings poem

I am a...
Acro dancer
Dog lover
Science lover
Purple lover
Good big sister
Yoga lover
McDonald's lover
Snake lover
Chocolate lover
And finally...
Winter lover.

Ella Peters (9)
Crazies Hill CE Primary School, Wargrave

This Is Me
A kennings poem

I am a...
Pig dreamer
Football hater
Chicken chaser
Non sleeper
Evil unicorn lover
Minecraft player
Video gamer
Nature lover
And finally...
TV watcher!

Ben Webster (8)
Crazies Hill CE Primary School, Wargrave

This Is Me

I am as loud as an elephant
I am as weird as a monkey
I am a pizza lover
I don't have a brother
I am as funny as a clown
I am as cool as a ninja.

Isla-Jean Preece (9)
Crazies Hill CE Primary School, Wargrave

This Is Me

I am a bookworm
I am a young zoologist
My second best friend is not human
My favourite animal is a wolf
I am protecting wildlife
This is me!

Jason Bennett (8)
Crazies Hill CE Primary School, Wargrave

This Is Me

A kennings poem

I am a...
Creative maker
Game player
Dog lover
Lego designer
Doodle drawer
Happy keeper.

Peter Sly (7)
Crazies Hill CE Primary School, Wargrave

This Is Me
A kennings poem

I am a...
Pizza eater
Snake lover
Underwater swimmer
Makes games
Lego designer.

Mario Tong (8)
Crazies Hill CE Primary School, Wargrave

You Created Me!

Strong mind, super kind
With a little sprinkle of sarcasm to make it all rhyme
I may be tiny in size, but don't mess with me!
Or you end might up finding yourself on the wrong side!
I like to have fun every day specifically on my PlayStation
And out and about in the day
I was born in March, didn't you see
My zodiac sign is an Aries!
I like to take a bath every day
So leave me alone when I'm showering, okay
I'm creepy enough to be Halloween
I love playing video games
All the same sports is my game
I did not write two poems, okay
But I love picking a racket
Hitting some squash balls outside of school
I wish they would fly 100mph.

Tariq Tandjiora (10)
East Peckham Primary School, East Peckham

Recipe Of Me

To create me, you will need:
Two handfuls of shyness and quietness
Five handfuls of friendliness
Ten handfuls of energy
Two cups of craziness
Twelve handfuls of weirdness
Twelve cups of happiness and creativity

To make me, you will need to:
Add two handfuls of shy and quiet into a bowl
With five handfuls of friendliness
And ten handfuls of energy
Stir while adding twelve handfuls of weirdness
And twelve cups of happiness and creativity
Bake for one hour.

Esther Brown (10)
East Peckham Primary School, East Peckham

How To Make Me!

To create me, you will need:
A house of really cute cats
A splash of shyness
Two cups of kindness
A cup of calmness
A splash of chattiness
A pinch of tiredness
A sprinkle of fun
A dash of helpfulness

Now you need to:
Add two cups of kindness
Mix a dash of helpfulness
Stir in a pinch of tiredness
Next, add a house of really cute cats
And a sprinkle of shyness
Add a splash of chattiness
Mix in a cup of calmness
Stir in a spoonful of fun

Spread the mix neatly over a tray of baking paper
Cook until glazed and fun-filled bubbles can
be seen
And leave to cool
This is me!

Evie Cooper (10)
East Peckham Primary School, East Peckham

This Is Me!

Caring and kind
Super-fast mind
I love to game
When I lose
I'm in pain
I'm pretty funny
My favourite animal is not a bunny
My favourite hobby is art
My dog always goes, "Bark!"
I have pretty eyes
They're like the colour of the sky
My favourite food is pizza and pasta
I would love to go see NASA
Polka-dot freckles
All fun and speckled
I love to listen to music
I shout, "Let's do this!"
I like school
It's pretty cool
I love watching movies

Some are quite groovy
This is me!

Emily Bastable (10)
East Peckham Primary School, East Peckham

This Is Me

I'm Thomas and I like Fortnite
I'm going to make a TikTok tonight
I like food, games and I like to sleep
I want to get driven around in a Jeep
I've got really long, lush hair and people stare
I don't like how people are polluting the air
I'm a really good sketcher and all my friends know that
My favourite animals are foxes and bats
I'm a Five Nights at Freddy's fanboy and my best friend is too
My baby sister has just turned two
This is me.

Thomas Fox (11)
East Peckham Primary School, East Peckham

I'm Not Telling You About Me

I really love gaming
And eating KFC
I don't like other people
And I don't think they like me

I like to go for walks
I quite like eating toast
But lying in my bed all day
Is what I like the most

My name starts with a T
I'm not telling you anymore
I've got silky hair and freckles.
That's enough about me.

Thomas Woodhams (10)
East Peckham Primary School, East Peckham

All About Horses...

I am giving love for horses
I am able to take them over courses

I am able to give treats to horses
I am sometimes having to use forces

I am giving care for horses
I am able to keep clean their water sources

I am good at riding horses
I am all about horses!

My name is Abigail
And my horse is called Brandy!

Abigail Hearn (10)
East Peckham Primary School, East Peckham

My Little Sister

I love my little sister
Because she's small and cute
She makes me laugh
When she giggles, laughs and shouts
My little sister is tiny but strong
When she goes to sleep
She always makes a thud with her feet
Even though I am only ten
I will love my little sister to the end.

Abel Thomas (10)
East Peckham Primary School, East Peckham

I Am...

I am blonde
I am James Bond
I am a brother
I am the Flash
I am the Hulk
I am smart
I am small
I am a cat lover
I am as kind as a kitten
I am as energetic as a puppy
I am the best gamer in the world
I am a mathematician
I am a best friend
This is me.

George Ridley (10)
East Peckham Primary School, East Peckham

This Is Me

I am a runner
I run like a cheetah
I am a boxer
I slip and roll
I am a footballer
I tackle and use my skills
I am speedy
I am a brother
I am a good brother
I am strong
I am as strong as the Hulk
I am a son
I am a fabulous son!

Archie Wilson (10)
East Peckham Primary School, East Peckham

This Is Me

T iny and short
H appiness in my smile
I love to draw and read
S ometimes I go into my garden

I love my family
S mart in some subjects

M essiness in my bedroom
E xcited all the time.

Poppy Jones (10)
East Peckham Primary School, East Peckham

This Is Me

T all as a tree
H appy like a dog
I gnorant like a bird
S mart like a teacher

I ntelligent like a dolphin
S hy like a dog

M essy like a monkey
E xcited like a baby puppy.

Sophie Webb (11)
East Peckham Primary School, East Peckham

This Is Me!

I am a bookworm
I am a money spender
I am a cuddle bear
I am a pasta eater
I am a smartypants (sometimes)
I am kind
I am funny
I am a crazy cat girl
I am weird (sometimes)
I am Lena Elizabeth Hedwig Geehan!

Lena Geehan (11)
East Peckham Primary School, East Peckham

Me

I am a kid
Not a lid
I love to game
But I'm not lame
I love meat
But I don't get beat
I am a winner
Not a gorilla
I don't get worried
But I love curry
I am fearless
Not gearless.

Ethan Coleman (10)
East Peckham Primary School, East Peckham

All About Me!

A kennings poem

Car lover
Ramp jumper
Bike racer
Art drawer
Silly laugher
Food muncher
Lego builder
Master gamer
Xbox obsessor
Running racer
Mayhem maker
Riddle solver
Teddy hugger
Joke teller
Telly watcher
Dog owner
Cat snuggler
Long walker
Silly brother
Hoodie wearer

Drink guzzler
Major explorer
Book reader.

Arthur R (10)
Eccleston St Mary's CE Primary School, Eccleston

Fantastic Facts About Freya
A kennings poem

Sloth lover
Noodle slurper
Family carer
Hip hop dancer
Friend hugger
Phone obsessor
Maggie snuggler
Primark desirer
Secret keeper
Fabulous supporter
Horrendous singer
Day dreamer
Great biker
Time teller
Audiologist admirer.

Freya W (10)
Eccleston St Mary's CE Primary School, Eccleston

Grace The Great

A kennings poem

Chocolate obsessor
Dog whisperer
Friendship giver
Trouble maker
Manchester United supporter
Pizza gobbler
Art lover
Animal admirer
Cake addict
Sausage nibbler
Onion hater
Sweet gulper
Frog adorer
Football player.

Grace R (10)
Eccleston St Mary's CE Primary School, Eccleston

Lillia The Great

A kennings poem

Technology lover
Marvel watcher
Skateboard rider
McDonald's gobbler
Sweet eater
Holiday obsessor
Hamster adorer
Dog cuddler
Sleeping machine
Art treasurer.

Lillia Marsden (10)
Eccleston St Mary's CE Primary School, Eccleston

About Me

A kennings poem

Chocolate gobbler
Horse rider
Tomato hater
Dog trainer
Bike rider
Phone addict
Dog walker
Pizza stuffer
Animal obsessor
Ice cream licker
Dog snuggler.

Holly McLaughlin (10)
Eccleston St Mary's CE Primary School, Eccleston

Magnificent Mia
A kennings poem

Dog lover
Allstar cheerleader
Tea slurper
Ariana Grande admirer
Chocolate chomper
Noodle slurper
Brother fighter
Friends obsessor
Mischief maker.

Mia Watson (10)
Eccleston St Mary's CE Primary School, Eccleston

All About Me!
A kennings poem

Sports addict
Game lover
Sweet gobbler
Bike rider
Mischief maker
Liverpool obsessor
Animal carer
McDonald's muncher
Chicken nugget devourer.

Matthew C (10)
Eccleston St Mary's CE Primary School, Eccleston

About Me
A kennings poem

Gymnastic lover
Problem solver
Food muncher
Book reader
Friendship spreader
Positive thinker
Animal liker
Fair player
Chocolate gobbler.

Mia Dodoo (10)
Eccleston St Mary's CE Primary School, Eccleston

Amazing Information About Me
A kennings poem

Football matcher
Fortnite player
Maths solver
PS obsessor
FIFA gamer
Pizza muncher
Riddle solver
Quick learner
Goofy brother.

Alex K (10)
Eccleston St Mary's CE Primary School, Eccleston

King Lucas
A kennings poem

Pizza muncher
Carbonara slurper
Space lover
Lego maker
Video game player
Crazy cat admirer
Star gazer
Day dreamer.

Lucas B (10)
Eccleston St Mary's CE Primary School, Eccleston

What Makes Me, Me
A kennings poem

Pet owner
Giraffe lover
Outside enjoyer
Tomato muncher
Food hoarder
Music approver
Puppy snuggler
Chaos causer.

Ava Juliette Craghill (10)
Eccleston St Mary's CE Primary School, Eccleston

All About Me
A kennings poem

Chocolate adorer
Dog owner
Music lover
Art maker
Ice lolly muncher
Game player
Rammstein admirer.

Kate Jackson (10)
Eccleston St Mary's CE Primary School, Eccleston

Hopes And Dreams

I hope, I hope to find this now,
I hope, I hope to make it somehow,
High spirits, dreams and many more I what I hope for,
A task to complete and victory to meet,
Is what I will adore.
Something to achieve and me finally becoming me,
Is what I will soar for.
I'm on the runaway, to find the achievement I made,
A daring adventure where I can venture and stay aware of all the hope.
All the hope that ravishingly floats through thick, humid air.
I hope I hope to find this now,
I hope, I hope to make it somehow.

Laila Youssef (11)
Edward Wilson Primary School, Westminster

The Recipe Of Me

Here's a girl that will give you a recipe of herself, 123
Bags of honesty,
Bags of curiosity,
Lots of bags of love and kindness,
10 bags of black scarves,
14 bags of perseverance,
9 bags of hard-working,
Bags of happiness,
8 bags of sportiness,
Bags of creativity,
Bags of a positive mindset,
5 bags of books,
Bags for ice cream and yummy foods.
This is a bit about me,
When the sun is shining,
I'm as happy as a jewel,
9 bags of the colour white and nude.
Jewellery too!

Zubaydah Aktar (10)
Edward Wilson Primary School, Westminster

All About Me

This poem is all about me,
First things first I like literacy,
I enjoy art and maths,
But the thing is, I am not good at that.

When I am at home, I am really lazy,
So I don't fall and be called clumsy,
All I do is rest, rest, rest,
Until I hear the alarm.
East-west food is the best!

I like the colour cyan, which is like blue,
I don't have patience so I can't stand in a queue.
I love nature, really like books,
But something I want is good looks!

Yousif Qazizada (10)
Edward Wilson Primary School, Westminster

What I Want To Be

I want to be a skilful and swift football player
I want to be an adventurous soul, pondering about life's mysteries
As much as I want to be a popular football player
Another thing I would like to be is an intellectual, knowledgeable scientist
My favourite colour is green, it's vibrant but also can be a dark colour
I like the colour green because it is tropical just like palm trees
I like calm and peace with a field of birds chatting.

Hassan Ali (10)
Edward Wilson Primary School, Westminster

Poem About Me

Hi! my name is Emily,
I like to read I like to draw!
I even like to eat,
When I grow up,
I would like to be an actress!
When I am sad I like to talk,
My eyes are as brown as solid dark,
My lips are the colour of peach,
Playing with my friends makes me happy,
I also really like being creative,
When I grow up,
I hope I get a mansion,
And have a happy life!

Emily Kaboli (10)
Edward Wilson Primary School, Westminster

My School Day

I came to school.
My friends are really cool
I've done some reading.
That's how I'm succeeding.
I do the daily mile.
Slow sometimes fast.
It helps me to focus in class.
Two times two is four.
Don't worry I know some more.
The dinner ladies are so kind.
I smile at them with a positive mind.
I'm doing mindfulness colouring.
Breathe in with my snout.
But oh no the fire alarm I've got to get out
Phew, it was just a drill now get up the stairs it feels like a hill.
Now it's time for science.
We have to be silent.
Now its time for the end of the day
At home, it's time to play.

Sabrina Khan (8)
Falconbrook Primary School, Battersea

Izzy Pop

I am kind and helpful to my friends every day.
Z ac and me are very best friends and that will never change.
Z arkish has a lot of knowledge and skills in learning in class,
Y ou are all great and so am I and isn't that great.

P opular people are great but think about other people like me and my friends.
O ver-excited children in Falconbrook or other schools having fun at school.
P eople with glorious smiles are me and Miss McGriven's thing indeed.

Ishrah Azgaoc (8)
Falconbrook Primary School, Battersea

I Am Very Sweet Like An Ice Cream

I am very sweet like an ice cream
Ice cream is as cold as an ice cube that melts like me on a hot day playing every day
Creamy, sweet and easy to eat
Chocolate and vanilla are my favourite dreamer
Looking forward every weekend to making ice cream by my hand
The recipe, I keep in my head and that makes me happy
When I have ice cream in my school it makes me glad when I don't, it makes me sad.

Sofia Porto (8)
Falconbrook Primary School, Battersea

Oh, Butterfly

Butterfly, butterfly,
Red, green and blue,
Don't leave me otherwise I'll be mad
But butterfly, sit on the flower and make me happy,
Oh, butterfly.

Iman Asif (8)
Falconbrook Primary School, Battersea

My Favourite Things

Sleeping, oh the best thing ever
Whenever I get home from school I'm asleep
I love sleep, it's the best
Sleep is my #1 best friend

On my birthday, my family got me a football
As soon as I got it, I started practising with it
Everyone likes it, especially my grandad
We all love football

Drawing, oh what a dream
Whenever I'm drawing it relieves my stress
Drawing makes me feel calm at times
When I'm mad
Sometimes I feel like I've got wings
When I'm drawing

Singing makes me
Feel like I'm growing up but I'm not
Sometimes singing makes me feel as free as a bird
Whenever I'm worried about something
I feel like singing
Singing is the love of my life

Meerkats are my favourite animal
Whenever I go to the zoo
I always rush to the meerkats
Meerkats always taunt me
It's like they can read my mind
This is my dream world.

Chloe Ramsay (10)
Hazelbury Primary School, Edmonton

This Is Me

I love Netflix, it has Trollhunters
Cobra Kai and even anime
I love Trollhunters
I have dreams of being
A trollhunter and using Merlin's amulet
Yeah, the ancient Merlin
I would have to save my school
From the savage brute, Gunmar
Leo had an amulet too
He was fighting Angor Rot
We won but I was unconscious

Cobra Kai is a very sad and very cool series
It's very sad because a kid named Miguel Diaz
Was kicked off the stairs in high school
He went into a coma
And woke up about a couple of weeks later
And was betrayed by his friends

Anime is the saddest of them all
It has a lot of deaths so that's why it's sad
You have to go on to websites or Netflix to watch

Naruto is my favourite
It may not be educational, but at least it's cool.
Nicholas Lambrou (11)
Hazelbury Primary School, Edmonton

Angry

Anger is that feeling that finds you anywhere you are
Anger is that feeling that controls your body at any time
Anger is that feeling that makes steam that comes out of your ears
Anger is that feeling that makes you want vengeance

Anger is that feeling that makes you want to hurt people
Anger is that feeling that makes your face and ears go red
Anger is that feeling that other people fear
Anger is that feeling that doesn't like happiness or optimism

Anger is that feeling that doesn't like to be around people
Anger doesn't like other emotions... like nervous

Anger is a rage and a rage is an anger
Anger is an uncontrollable emotion that you can't stop.

Leo Mensah (10)
Hazelbury Primary School, Edmonton

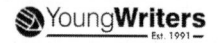

Up Above!

When people think of us
They think we're immortal
They think we're cool
But down below, we're a living ghost

Down below, football makes me happy
I like poems, I hope you like them too
This poem is about me
I like tag rugby and I like dodgeball too

Sport is everywhere it can be in your home
Playing ball is restricted
Sport is, sport does
Sports for me is the whole world
Sport does, sport is
I want vengeance when I lose the match

Vengeance is what I want when I play and lose
Moaning and struggling as I came off the pitch
The pitch waved bye-bye.

Cairo Roberts-Dabner (10)
Hazelbury Primary School, Edmonton

Adventurous Me

Adventurous me, up and down
Brave and calm till it's dark
Mountains are big and colossal
As time flies like a flash

Adventurous me, up and down
Brave and calm till it's dark
Camping up on a mountain
Looking up as the moon glistened brightly

Adventurous me, up and down
Brave and calm till it's dark
As the wind blows gently
And I can hear rustling trees
I wonder what it could be?

Adventurous me, up and down
Brave and calm till it's dark
As I go further up the mountain
I feel present breathing
Thinking who could it be?

Mumtaz Mohamed (11)
Hazelbury Primary School, Edmonton

Things That Make Me Feel Myself

T hings that make me
H appiness passes by and it makes me remember life is great and everyone should enjoy it
I love to practice my handwriting
S ometimes I like drawing but it's not my passion

I love to eat
S cience teaches me things I never knew about

M usic makes me feel happy and relaxed
E nglish is my hobby

P assion is a strong feeling in your heart
O h, I forgot...
E ating is my hobby
M y last thing is my friends, they always make me smile when I am down.

Mikayla Morgan (11)
Hazelbury Primary School, Edmonton

Up Above

When people think of up above
They think of heaven
But I say it's never-ending
Me and my friends always look up to the stars
Or is it never-ending?

My life is bizarre they surround me
Like I'm a real-life superstar!
I wish life was never-ending
But eventually, I will be never-ending

It sounds crazy but it's like gravy
You feel warm and smug
When they surround you
It feels like they're your own compound

When people think of up above
They think of heaven
But I say it's never-ending.

Jayden Moore (10)
Hazelbury Primary School, Edmonton

Things I Love

Anime is a type of movie or series you can watch
But make sure it's for your age
BTS is the kind of music that you can listen and vibe to
Calling lets you speak to anybody who is far away on a mobile

Food! Yum!
It's the tastiest thing you have ever seen
and tasted
Everyone loves food, right?
Sleeping!
Sleeping is the best!

Happy stuff could make you mad as well, but it's all fine
Other people like different things
Some people are silly, some people are serious
Everybody's personalities are different.

Tiana K N Kironde (10)
Hazelbury Primary School, Edmonton

Books! Books! Books!

Books hold stories that engage you to fall into
Books hold secrets hidden in the lines, as if under disguise
Books, non-fiction or fantasy, are jam-packed with adventure
Just awaiting you to peek and venture

Books hold the darkest stories
The weirdest secrets waiting to be unveiled
It intends to change your perspective
The theories left to bounce in your head

Books leave you waiting in awe
Wanting you to venture in once more
Books engross you, it's true
Soon it'll inspire you, just like me.

Nafisa Mohamed (10)
Hazelbury Primary School, Edmonton

Nightmares

Nightmares force you to scream
A nightmare is a blood-curdling dream
It sends worries and shivers down your spine
Just like Jack climbing down a vine

After a nightmare, you wake up sweating
I don't know how but you start regretting
You sweat, you will be aghast
These are nightmares, some make you feel
Abashed!

Some nightmares are of long, slender fingers
Travelling up and around your face
Others are of poverty or a sign of bad luck

These are nightmares
You might have them.

Kavya Matadar (10)
Hazelbury Primary School, Edmonton

Optimistic

Happy is like the op to the mistic
Don't be unrealistic
I'm just looking at the statistics
Optimistic is the thing
Keeping your head up high
On the darkest nights

Optimistic is the emotion
That everybody likes
It's the opposite of taking hikes
Optimism is like a train
You keep going and going
You want it again and again

Music is the thing
That makes me optimistic
But everybody is individualistic
This is just me.

Raul Poara (10)
Hazelbury Primary School, Edmonton

Emotions

Emotions are any kind of feelings
But sometimes they're unappealing
Most of the time, they're misleading

Emotions are anything you want them to be
Most of the time, people disagree
I just want to tie the bad emotions to a tree
In that case, they want to flee

Emotions, you can be silly, angry or even snappy
My favourite is to be happy
When I'm happy or silly, I jump all over the place
I scream into a pillow when I'm angry or snappy.

Lola Warne (10)
Hazelbury Primary School, Edmonton

Going To Space

I dreamt about going to space
After so many years, I made it
I was going to space
Then I thought it was a dream
To the future
I flew away from Earth

I woke up in the year 3033!
I was in the future
I saw floating, strong cars
I was safe... just for now...

Omer Muhammed Sanci (11)
Hazelbury Primary School, Edmonton

This Is Me

Crazy but chilled,
If you don't wanna be killed,
Don't mess with me,
When I am tired or you will just have to wait and see.

Bold but smart,
Not so good at art,
I'm a dog lover,
And a passionate footballer.

On the pitch 24/7,
I play for two teams and that's my heaven,
Football is my sport,
And I am lightning bolt sprinting fast the ones who are short.

Game in the night,
Sometimes I get a fright,
Game in the day,
That's my way.

So this is me,
My lunatic friends will help me even when I'm silly,
Rarely sad, maybe a bit mad,
A bit untidy but that's just me nothing so bad.

Ella Basherville (10)
King Edward Primary School, North Shields

This Is Me

I'm simply sporty,
I'm an incredible ice-skater,
Horses are for life,
I'm a terrific tennis player,
This is me!

I have the skills,
That'll give you the chills,
I like to cook cakes,
Take a look at my milkshakes.

I'm an animal adorer,
I have a playful puppy,
My favourite animal is fluffy,
It's a highland cow!
This is me!

I am fantastically fearless,
I'm also adventurous,
I can be tentative,
But I'm never argumentative,
This is me!

As I said I'm very chilled,
And I have the skills,
I love art,
And I love pop tarts,
This is me!

Juliette Herzberg (11)
King Edward Primary School, North Shields

Beware Of The Girl

B eware of the girl, short with reddish-brown hair
I ntelligence level average and terrified of bears
L ack of comfort while trying to sleep
L ittle do her cats know, they make more noise than a peep
I n love, Minecraft loves her friends even more.
E ager to get home, to appear at my mum's door.

P oppy day celebration
I s good at alliteration
C ar made for seven
K eeps waiting for the day she'll be eleven
L over for animals of any kind
E xcited on the daily hope you don't mind
S o be careful of the girl with reddish-brown hair.

Billie Pickles (10)
King Edward Primary School, North Shields

How To Create Me

To create a Florance Chambers you will need:
A box of arts and crafts.
A dash of boldness.
A dollop of spicy chicken wings, and Ramen noodles.
A sprinkle of style
A plop of anime, Minecraft and Roblox.
A sliver of silliness.
And a slab of frogs, snakes and axolotls.

Now you need to:
Preheat the oven to the high temperature and cook me on low confidence,
After 20 mins take me out and place me on a sofa where I can chill and play video games.
Then wait for me to cook at low loudness temperature.
Once done, top me with a sausage roll and sweet chilli sauce.
This is me.

Florence Chambers (10)
King Edward Primary School, North Shields

The Confident Boy

I am a lightning bolt in football boots,
I am a sporty skilled,
I am a lover of my dog, Daisy is the best,
I am a fantastic fabulous football player,
I am as passionate as a coach,
My family is as loving as a lion and its cub,
My hair is as brown as a bear and my eyes always feel like they are going to fall out,
I am a lazy sleeper.

I am an anxious stresser and as emotional as losing a world cup final,
I am a curious mathematician and an adventurous explorer,
I am as competitive as a professional footballer,
This is me.

Sebastian Knowles (11)
King Edward Primary School, North Shields

How To Make Me!

To create me you will need:
A bucket full of fun
A dash of brightness
A pinch of awesome
10g of book worms
A sprinkle of sweetness
One artistic and calm mind
100g of happiness.

Now you need to:
Add a bucket full of fun,
Then put in a pinch of awesome.
Stir jaggedly while adding in a dash of brightness,
Next, add 10g of bookworms,
Add a sprinkle of sweeteners,
Mix in one artistic and calm mind,
Finally, add 100g of happiness,
Put into oven for 1 hour on temperature 180.
This is me.

Matilda Ironside (10)
King Edward Primary School, North Shields

The Footballer

I am a lightning bolt in football boots,
I'm a dog lover, I love Murphy the English Springer.
Murphy is the best.
I love football,
I'm a superstar striker,
I like to think I'm funny but I don't know if people are just laughing at me,
I am a wolf, strong and fearless,
I'm fabulously fun,
I'm amazingly awesome,
I'm spectacularly sporty,
And I'm super smart,

My hair is gold, blonde and white,
My eyes are swirls of brown mist,
My skin is tanned,
This is me.

Katie Dixon (10)
King Edward Primary School, North Shields

This Is Me

To create me you will need:
A bedroom full of craziness
10lbs of loving dogs
One pinch of fashion
A bag full of loving chocolate
A few sprinkles of fun.

Now you need to:
Put the bedroom full of craziness in a bowl with a touch of McDonald's.
Next, add 10lbs of loving dogs and a bag full of loving chocolate in the bowl.
Add a few sprinkles of fun,
Bake at 100 for 20 minutes and you have successfully made me!

Beau Heslop (10)
King Edward Primary School, North Shields

My Name Is Connie - A Rap Poem

Curious, chilled and kind.
I'm sweet and sour,
Depending on the hour,
Helpful and nice,
Angry and lazy.

I'm as slow as a sloth,
But a lightning bolt in football.
Arts, crafts, drawing,
That's my passion.

Chatty in my house,
Shy in school.
Always smiling,
Angry sometimes.

Here are some facts about me.
My dream job is,
Photography.
My eyes are as blue
As the sky.

My name is,
Connie.

Connie Culyer (10)
King Edward Primary School, North Shields

My Favourite Football Team

We look chilled but our wingers are menacing,
On the attack, we're proposing,
Our best player has the skills,
And he'll give you the chills,
Our mascot is a magpie so were black and white,
Premier League or Championship we don't care,
We'll take it and pride with it we shall wear!
And just to top it off we have the richest owners,
Now, none of our fans will be moaners.

Answer: Newcastle.

Joshua Burgon (10)
King Edward Primary School, North Shields

Me

I am a great gamer champ,
But it's hard to be because of my little brother who likes to stamp.
Art is my power!
But maths makes me cower.

I run, I jump
That's all I need to get five mins to myself only
I do kick-boxing to attack my brother in the face,
But the thing is that after that he looks a disgrace!
I love basketball, I dribble, pretty fast,
But a Saturday beach fire is what I save last.

Asa Mather (11)
King Edward Primary School, North Shields

Recipes

To create me you will need:
A salad sandwich
A piece of hot chocolate
7lbs of sportiness
A spoon of happiness
A bullet of brightness
A cupcake of fun.

Now you need to:
Add a sprinkle of enjoyment.
In case the temperature
Decrease some energetics and silliness.
Add 2lbs of sugar.
Add some sprinkles like a cake for enjoyment.
Some exercise and smiles.

Hamzah Islam (10)
King Edward Primary School, North Shields

My Autumn

Autumn is a season I love,
My hat, scarf and glove,
Trudging through crunchy leaves,
It just makes me smile with glee.

I like to adventure and play.
Out through the autumn day,
The cold breeze slips my fingers,
Autumn lingers.

Running along an icy street,
My friend I see who I like to meet,
Fingertips numb and cold,
My palms, red and very bold.

Alexandra Dunn (10)
King Edward Primary School, North Shields

This Is Me

I am a messy monster,
I am a wave of worry,
I am a tremendous tennis player,
I am as curious as an adventurous explorer,
I am a bonkers book worm,
My friends describe me as a silly sausage,
I am a vast engineer,
I am a fabulous football fan,
I am crazy competitive,
I am a video game king,
I am a passionate person,
This is me.

Archie Duckworth (10)
King Edward Primary School, North Shields

This Is Me

I am a fabulous footballer,
I am a tiger strong and brave,
I am as annoying as an alarm clock,
I am a curious explorer,
I am an animal lover,
My eyes are sparkly blue marbles,
My hair is blonde like the sunshine,
I am a video game lord,
I am easily bored,
I can be sweet I can be sour depending on the hour!
This is me!

Liam Grant (11)
King Edward Primary School, North Shields

Jack's Poem

I'm happy, I'm sad,
Depending on the hour.
Sometimes I make a crowd,
Sometimes I make silence.

A goal I celebrate, I'm a sporty kid.
I am a super footy fan,
I go to London whenever I can.

Generous, kind and a super-fast mind.
Maths and English is my superpower,
But French makes me cower.

Jack Cullerton-White
King Edward Primary School, North Shields

How To Make Me

You need;
100lb of fun
20lb of stupidness
A pinch of chilled
A bucket of energy
Handful of mischief.

Now you need to:
Mix it with a pinch of chilled
Add a bucket of energy
20lb of stupidness and mix
Finally, add a hand full of mischief and you are done.

Lucas Armstrong (10)
King Edward Primary School, North Shields

This Is Me

I'm helpful but clumsy,
But a little bit bossy.
I am cheeky but chilled
And my mind is filled.

I am curious and kind,
I have a super mind.
Football is fantastic,
And sometimes I'm charismatic.

I'm also crazy,
And yes I'm also called Maisie.

Maisie Heskett (10)
King Edward Primary School, North Shields

Who Is It?

Guess the person:

Bright blue eyes with a dash of blonde-brown hair,
A passionate, smart, chilled boy ready for anything to hit him.
Funny, happy but sometimes crazy. But not silly.
Not a very sporty person.
Likes to sit and chill.

Have you got him?
He's me!

Alfie Taylor (10)
King Edward Primary School, North Shields

This Is Me

T all.
H air is as blonde as golden sand.
I ce blue is my favourite colour.
S ophie is my best friend.

I love to dance.
S illy and sporty.

M y sisters make me laugh.
E merald green eyes that shine in the seawater.

Sara Turnbull (10)
King Edward Primary School, North Shields

This Is Me

This is me,
Sporty and kind,
This is me,
An easy person to find.

A football lover,
Chilled and messy,
A passionate gamer,
I'm almost always friendly.

A brave boy,
Adventurous and courageous,
A secret keeper,
I am never outrageous.

Zach Cottingham (11)
King Edward Primary School, North Shields

This Is Me

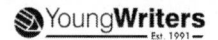

T his is me
H air as blonde as a sandy beach,
I cy blue eyes,
S illy and energetic.

I 'm kind helpful and happy
S miley and smart.

M y favourite colour is purple
E very animal is my favourite.

Olivia Gregg (10)
King Edward Primary School, North Shields

This Is Me!

I am fearless
I am not afraid of the dark
I am brilliant at maths
I am good at games
I am good at basketball
I am a hamster and dog lover
I am fast as a cheetah
I am good at votes
I am happy all the time
I am an apple eater.

Liam Nicholson (11)
King Edward Primary School, North Shields

This Is Me

I love dogs
I chop logs
I can't sing absolutely anything!
I love games with flames
I am funny like a bunny
I want to act like a cat
I want to scare like a bear
I don't care, what you say, I'm not leaving
This is me!

Joshua Rutherford (11)
King Edward Primary School, North Shields

I Am A...

A kennings poem

I am a...
Tree climber
Wasp fleer
Guinea pig owner
Adventure seeker
Hockey dreamer
Pizza lover
Chocolate eater
Story writer
Friend to most!
But last but not least
A great helper.

Amy Dillon (10)
King Edward Primary School, North Shields

This Poem Is Me

Meet me,
Happy but sad,
Lazy but adventurous,
Sweet eater and mischief leader,
Smart and messy,
Acrobatic goalkeeper like bricks pilled up on the line,
Fearsome and bold,
Angry but friendly.

Jake Beavers (10)
King Edward Primary School, North Shields

I Am...
A kennings poem

I am an...
Adventure lover
Kickboxer
Bike rider
Early riser
Strong boxer
Curious explorer
Cat and dog lover
Sweet eater
And finally...
Chilled out.

Archie Brown (11)
King Edward Primary School, North Shields

This Is Me!
A kennings poem

I am a...
Football player
Crisp eater
Dance lover
Light sleeper
Nandos eater
Dog lover
Late sleeper
Cheeky chatter
And finally
A good helper.

Polly Binks (10)
King Edward Primary School, North Shields

This Is Me
A kennings poem

I am an...
Artist
Autumn wisher
Cake maker
Dog lover
Early riser
Halloween lover
McDonald's eater
Normal sleeper
Finally
I'm just me.

Faith Callaghan (10)
King Edward Primary School, North Shields

This Is Me

I am a...
Horse rider
Dancer
Animal lover
Adventurous person
Chocolate eater
Sporty
Fearless
Quite organised
Very energetic
Early riser.

Luisa Gray (11)
King Edward Primary School, North Shields

How To Make Me!

To make me, you need:
Lots of maths
A pinch of games
Pizza
Rabbits
A tray
Oven
Teddies
Cuter teddies

G aming salt needs to go on the tray
A nd then add the cute teddies in
M ake an even cuter teddy and put it
I n the tray. Then put in a pizza and maths
N ext, add even more maths and cook in the oven
G et out the tray and you have me!

Isaac Franks (8)
Kingswood Parks Primary School, Kingswood

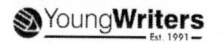

How To Make Me

You will need:
A cup of annoyance
A bucket of chatter
An empty cup of shyness
A truck full of books

Pour in the cup of annoyance and mix it
While mixing, chuck in a bucket of chatter
Throw away the empty cup
Go outside and get some books
Put it in the oven
And that's how you make me.

Naomi Skorczewski (9)
Kingswood Parks Primary School, Kingswood

A Recipe About Me

To make me, you will need:
A bowl
A cup full of confidence
A spoonful of mischief
A little bit of jelly and ice cream
And chocolate cake
Also friendship
A bit of football

Put them all in the bowl
And mix them together
Then put it in the oven
This is me!

Amelia W (10)
Kingswood Parks Primary School, Kingswood

This Is Me

T uesday is my favourite day
H appiness makes the world a better place
I love football
S ummer is the best

I love running
S miles are contagious

M y bedroom needs books
E veryone should love to read.

Gracie C (8)
Kingswood Parks Primary School, Kingswood

This Is Me

My hair is as wavy as water streaming
through a forest
My eyes are like emerald marbles
My skin is like smooth and wet petals
My lips are the colour of red roses
And as soft as a pilow
My eyes are as round as marbles
And as sparkly as diamonds.

Vanesa C (8)
Kingswood Parks Primary School, Kingswood

All About Me

T his is me
H ats are fashionable
I' m not a girly girl
S ummer makes me smile

I love football and space
S quash is my game

M argarita pizza is yummy
E dee is my name.

Edee Frankie Silvester (8)
Kingswood Parks Primary School, Kingswood

This Is Me

T his is my favourite poem
H ate broccoli
I love cake
S oup is my favourite

I love Pokémon
S illy is my nickname for my brother

M eat is good food
E llie is my friend.

Ivy B (8)
Kingswood Parks Primary School, Kingswood

To Create Me, You Need...

To create me, you need:
Some sunlight
Some happiness
Some joy
Some carrots
Some chocolate
Some love

Mix together
And put in the oven for twenty minutes
Give it another mix
Then eat it!

Grace Gill Howard (7)
Kingswood Parks Primary School, Kingswood

Animals

A eroplanes are my favourite way to travel
N uggets I love to eat
I love bunnies
M eatballs are tasty
A dvent calenders I love
L ife is good
S ummer is a season I like.

Ella McGrath (9)
Kingswood Parks Primary School, Kingswood

How To Make Me

You will need:
A giant bed
Lots of kittens
A hot cheesy and stringy pizza
A big, big swing
Lots of Robux

Blend it all together
And add a little shimmer.

Maria Jackson (7)
Kingswood Parks Primary School, Kingswood

Still, I Am Me

When you are down you are happy to be you,
When you are ill you are still happy to be alive,
Still, I am me.
When you feel upside down you love to be you,
If you are scared you are worried but happy to be alive.
Still, I am me.
Still, I am me.
When you feel you cant do it you can do it,
Because it is in you.
Things just need thinking sometimes somethings need questions,
You have everything inside you, you just need to find it.
Still, I am me.

Jake Thompson (9)
Larks Hill J&I School, Pontefract

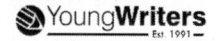

All About My Life

I am not for everyone
I know my truth I know who I am
I know what I do and do not bring
Being hurt only
Makes you grow
The more you know
Then try hard to gain
The best lessons are
Learnt through pain.

Mia Jocek (8)
Larks Hill J&I School, Pontefract

Olivia

O livia can be a cheeky girl,
L iv is what some people call her.
I am intelligent and bright.
V ibe is what I like
I make friends easily,
A nd this is the end of me!

Olivia Crompton (8)
Larks Hill J&I School, Pontefract

This Is Me

T he elephants and koalas are my favourite animals.
H opping rabbits are my pets, they're sisters and they're so cute and fluffy.
I love water so refreshing.
S weetcorn is so sweet and one of my favourite foods but my favourite food is a full English breakfast from Morrisons.

I n my house, I have two brothers, one sister and a mummy and daddy.
S ugary sweets are so good and tasty.

M y family and I watch a movie on Sundays
E mpathy is what I show and I never give up.

Darcy M (7)
Little Heaton CE Primary School, Rhodes

This Is Me

T hursday I go to Beavers every week
H appy Friday I get high fives
I like poppy flowers and my teddy Peter Rabbit.
S o every week on Friday I go swimming.

I go to school and everyone likes me
S weet lollies are my favourite food.

M y mum, dad and brother are the best
E veryone in the school is my friend.

Poppy Collins (7)
Little Heaton CE Primary School, Rhodes

This Is Me

T 'mia is my name
H appy I am when the sunshine
I s it just me or is something on my head?
S ome things in life are hard but I'll make it through.

I s that McDonald's? My favourite.
S ome people love vegetables but not me.

M y favourite animal is a cat
E veryone is my friend.

T'mia Uff (8)
Little Heaton CE Primary School, Rhodes

Kaggwa's Nintendo Poem

T oday I want a Nintendo Switch for Christmas.
H appy when it's my birthday when I am eight.
I n my house, I play games on my phone.
S undays my dad makes eggs.

I n school, I get a lot of dojos.
S o I never give up.

M y happy days are Fridays and Thursdays.
E yes black, hair black.

Kaggwa Mawanda (7)
Little Heaton CE Primary School, Rhodes

This Is Me

T hursdays at my school we have music
H appy when I call my friends
I hate my brother and sister a lot
S unflowers are planted all over my garden.

I want to go horse riding lessons
S ometimes I stroke my cat.

M ondays I go to swimming lessons
E very Saturday I go dancing.

Lilia Rogers (7)
Little Heaton CE Primary School, Rhodes

The Wonderful Things In My Life

T hursday I go swimming.
H appy I am when everybody is quiet.
I n the winter I love to stamp in leaves.
S now is my favourite when I make a snowman.

I n class, it is very loud.
S ometimes I annoy the teachers.

M y family is the best family.
E mmie is my best friend ever.

Renee Rogers (7)
Little Heaton CE Primary School, Rhodes

I'm Back

T oday I go swimming
H arper is my name
I am eight and crafty
S illy my friends call me.

I love DT and art
S o I'm bored let's go to the park because I love the park.

M mm, it's time for food now which is every sec!
E mmie, Sarach, Renee, and T'Mia.

Harper Smith (8)
Little Heaton CE Primary School, Rhodes

This Is Me

T omato is my favourite fruit
H appy playing with my teddys and my family friends
I ce cream is yummy and tasty
S andwiches are my tasty food

I like Halloween cake is tasty
S wimming every Fridays

M y favourite teddy is Mr Snuggles
E nd of my swimming lessons.

Annabelle Garrod (8)
Little Heaton CE Primary School, Rhodes

The Mixed-Up Poem

T oday I am playing computer games.
H appy when having ice cream.
I don't like playing with my brother,
S o I drink a milkshake instead.

I like football.
S ometimes I don't like scary noises.

M y lovely cousin.
E veryone is bad and good.

Leo Johnson (7)
Little Heaton CE Primary School, Rhodes

Mummy And Daddy

T omorrow I'm going on track stars.
H appy I'm playing among us.
I n my mum's house, I have two annoying brothers
S ometimes I eat Skittles

I am magic
S andy holidays are nice to go on

M y mummy is really sweet
E ach day I watch TV.

Cole Moore (8)
Little Heaton CE Primary School, Rhodes

Kylan's Poem

T omato game I like to play
H appy when I am playing outside
I ce cream is very tasty
S unny days I love going on my swing.

I love cake
S eeds I like to plant in my garden.

M y favourite food is chicken nuggets
E veryone thinks I am funny.

Kylan Roberts-Hall (7)
Little Heaton CE Primary School, Rhodes

Layla's Life

T hursdays I go to school.
H appy girls every day.
I love my teacher.
S unny days I like to chill out.

I 'm always good at school.
S o I never get put in the book.

M y life is great how it is.
E very day we have maths.

Layla King (7)
Little Heaton CE Primary School, Rhodes

Things About Me

T igers I love my favourite animal
H appy swimming I love this sport
I like eating KitKats
S ister is called Sylvie.

I hate cats
S IS bottles are what I drink from.

M um I love
E ggs my dad sometimes has for breakfast.

Jonah Holdsworth (7)
Little Heaton CE Primary School, Rhodes

I Like Cats And Sweets

T his is me I have a very cute cat
H e is so grey
I s my favourite animal
S weets are my favourite treat

I s my cat my favourite animal?
S ome people like me

M y favourite milkshake is strawberry
E njoy playing games.

Louis Trylski (7)
Little Heaton CE Primary School, Rhodes

Reggie

T his is my hobby
H appy I am most when I go to bed
I n my room I am boss
S weets are my favourite.

I n my house, I have two brothers
S weet dogs are the best.

M y favourite thing is KFC
E very day I drink Vimto.

Reggie Boyd (7)
Little Heaton CE Primary School, Rhodes

Ernest's Life

T uesdays I go to karate.
H ate my brother.
I mmediately annoyed.
S hame is by my side.

I naccurate bullet shot in games,
S neak, all the time.

M aybe I'll be rich one day.
E nvious of my brother every day.

Ernests Dreimanis (7)
Little Heaton CE Primary School, Rhodes

The Greatest Things That Happen Today

T omorrow I wake up.
H appy day everyone.
I t is a wonderful day.
S o it is school today.

I t is sunny outside.
S o it is school today.

M y life is great.
E verything is going great.

Millie Smith (8)
Little Heaton CE Primary School, Rhodes

This Is Me

Thursday I do English
Friday I set to pounce.
Happy Leighton I am;
Is my brother called Jamal?
Sweets are my favourite treat.
I am seven years old and I am strong.
Sometimes I eat McDonald's.
I like doing trick or treat with my friends.

Leighton Cleary (7)
Little Heaton CE Primary School, Rhodes

This Is Me

T hursday is wonderful
H appy girl happy every day
I love my mum
S ad I can be sometimes

I like dogs,
S ometimes I am really kind

M y friends are noisy
E very day I am smiley.

Emmie Irving (7)
Little Heaton CE Primary School, Rhodes

Things About Me

T oday it is Friday
H appy I am on my iPad
I n my house it is crazy
S weets are bad

I hate Michael
S arah is my BFF

M y mum is really nice
E ggs are disgusting.

Lilly Garrity (8)
Little Heaton CE Primary School, Rhodes

This Is Orla

My name is Orla
I am flexible because I love to dance,
exercise and I'm energetic.
A recipe of me is:
A jug of flexibility,
A spoonful of bubbly,
Needs more organisation,
Some smartness,
A drop of annoying,
A cup of friendly,
A load of smiles and
A cup of funny.
My dream for the future is to
either be a professional dancer
or a dance teacher.
One of my favourite things I love to do
Is walk my dog, Hugo.
One other thing I like to do
is go to the park with my friends.
I am as bouncy as a kangaroo or a frog
When I am sad, I like to ignore it and have fun

My favourite colour is rose-gold
And that is me, so I hope you like it.

Orla Downs (10)
Machanhill Primary School, Machanhill

All About Me

My name is Energetic Emily
I am ten years old
I live in Larkhall in Scotland
Sometimes I am annoying like my brother
A drop of loudness and happiness
My hobbies are playing football and drawing
When I was younger, a boy said to me
"Girls can't play football!"
But I proved them wrong
I have trained harder and harder each day
When I lose a match, I am sad and sometimes I cry
But I give my mum a hug and listen to music
Also, I play video games like Minecraft
Roblox and Fortnite with my friends
I also eat healthy food like fruit
Vegetables and some sweets.

Emily Fernon (10)
Machanhill Primary School, Machanhill

This Is Me

My name is Lexi
Likeable Lexi
I am friendly
I am happy
Sometimes I am kind
But we can't all be perfect
I am as small as a bean
Not as tall as a tree
My future is bright
I need to work hard to get to my future
I would like to do hair and nails
I know I can do good but people have their opinion

Let me tell you a recipe
It is two cups of silliness
A drizzle of always angry
And a jug of happiness and kindness
When I am sad, I talk to my mum and dad about it
So they can solve it out
You always need friends.

Lexi Guy (10)
Machanhill Primary School, Machanhill

This Is William

W hen I play football, I play with my friends
I am always outside playing football in the good weather
L ove when I play centre-midfield for my football team
L ove when I have KFC for my dinner
I like when I have football training at night-time
A m the kind of person that loves football
M y football career has been going for six months and I have scored twenty-five goals in nine matches in the league right now.

William Boyd (10)
Machanhill Primary School, Machanhill

Myself

As smart as a fox
As lazy as a box
As calm as the air
As funny as a bunny
As fast as a hare
As crazy as a bear
As colourful as a rainbow
And as nice as gold
I want to go to Korea
But I doubt I'll get to go there
I draw when I'm sad, then I cheer up a lot
I'll be an actor, no matter the cause
I'm as loud as an eagle
My eyes are like diamonds
And I'm done right there.

Aimee Newlands (9)
Machanhill Primary School, Machanhill

This Is Me

C aius is my name
A s cool as ice
I love my family
U nlikely to go to Canada
S neaky as a fox

I 'm kind and honest
A s warm as the sun
N ever give up

M y love for my family and friends is amazing
U ncruel
L ove
L ovely
E nergetic
N ice.

Caius Ian Mullen (10)
Machanhill Primary School, Machanhill

This Is Me

My name is Naomi
I am nice

A teaspoon of effort
A jug of excitement
A drip of annoying
A split of laughter
When I grow up, I want to be a hairdresser
Like my sister
When I am sad, my dad goes on a walk with me
We get ice cream
I like to do taekwondo
I like to do sparring
I think I am getting more fit.

Naomi Taylor (10)
Machanhill Primary School, Machanhill

This Is Me

My name is Sporty Sam
I am as healthy as a rabbit
I am as energetic is a cheetah
My dream is to be a fantastic football player

This is a recipe of me
A jar of impatient
A drop of annoyingness

When I am sad, I go for a walk
With my mum or dad into the woods
Also when I am sad, I have a nap.

Sam Bishop (10)
Machanhill Primary School, Machanhill

This Is Me

C ool as ice
H elpful
R eally fast
I like strawberries
S uper helpful
T ries to be good at math
O ld as ten
P lanned
H elpful
E xcellent at coding
R eading is my favourite.

CJ Hamilton (10)
Machanhill Primary School, Machanhill

This Is Me

I am happy as a dog
As silly as a chimp
And I'm fast on my bike
I love my friends and family
And I love playing with my dogs
As warm as the sun
A handful of funny
I love going to the woods
And I love going to the beach
My life is amazing.

Dylan Hunter (10)
Machanhill Primary School, Machanhill

All About Me

My name is Kirsten
I'm as strong as an ox
When I'm older, I want to be a zookeeper
Animals fascinate me
When I'm sad, I listen to music
I do Taekwondo
My favourite animal is a dog
Some people call me Kind Kirsten.

Kirsten Ferguson Walker (10)
Machanhill Primary School, Machanhill

This Is Me

My name is Coll Watson
I am as smart as a dog
I can share all my thoughts
I am as lazy as a sloth
I am as jumpy as a kangaroo
I am as annoying as a fly
I am angry as a hamster
I am as sneaky as a snake
I love lakes.

Coll Watson (9)
Machanhill Primary School, Machanhill

This Is Me

My name is Scarlett
I am nine years old
I love dogs and all animals
In the future, I want to be a dance
And running teacher
When I am sad, I like to chill and listen to music
I have a nickname; Scary Scarlett.

Scarlett Semple (9)
Machanhill Primary School, Machanhill

This Is Me!

P atient as a tiger
H as a touch of kindness
I s a little bit annoying
L ikes pizza a lot
I s very friendly
P hilip is my name.

Philip Spence (10)
Machanhill Primary School, Machanhill

This Is Me

My name is Kind Kayla
In the future, I want to live in Japan
In a beautiful house with my friends
Sasha and Aimee
I would like to work in a restaurant.

Kayla Rundell (10)
Machanhill Primary School, Machanhill

Wonderful Things That Make Me Happy

A beautiful day on the beach eating fish and chips with some bbq dips,
Then I had some sips of juice after we went to a nice arcade,
Then I played some games and won,
Exoctic prizes and more but after I headed to bed.

A cold day, gaming with a nice hot chocolate,
This is life, so should we roll the dice?
Ahh! Here's a mouse in the room while I'm trying to roll,
This game is super fun so all joy unfolds in every way possible.

A nice day playing football in the wet, slimy mud,
Have fun after we played
I get a moment to think about family and friends helping me come this far,
So we go celebrate in the house,
But the joy folds when one day you will retire.

Macorley Jevons (11)
Smith's Wood Primary Academy, Smith's Wood

Doll Cafe

I want to aspire, to be able to admire, my cafe in the street.
Let's serve tea, with cake and all,
Let's own a cafe with porcelain dolls along the walls.

Out of reach of danger, let's welcome in a fellow stranger,
We have made it to here, let's hear a cheer!
Nighttime rolls around, I've locked up the cafe.

As happy as can be, little old me.

Careful not to knock off the dolls!
A-ring-a-ding! Someone's here!
Feeling so excited, I'm so happy I've made it here.

Eyeing the dolls, not a speck of dust.
A cafe is an absolute must.

Gracie-Leigh Wood (10)
Smith's Wood Primary Academy, Smith's Wood

Delightful Demi - This Is Me

I have long brown hair,
I have eyes as brown as wood,
I have pretty pink circle glasses,
This is me.

I am a reliable, kind girl,
I am as smart as a genius scientist.
I am terrible at keeping secrets,
This is me.

I value someone who is trustworthy,
I value someone who could stand up for me,
I value someone who could never leave me heartbroken.
This is me.

I enjoy dancing and singing,
I love doing fun stuff in DT,
I like eating scrumptious,
Delicious food.
This is me.

Demi-Leigh Gouldingay (8)
Smith's Wood Primary Academy, Smith's Wood

Magical Mahrosh

I have black and brown hair,
I have black eyes as the dark,
I have beautiful dresses,
This is me.

I am a cool, awesome girl,
I am kind as Miss Boobyer,
I am calm and playful,
This is me.

I value someone who is kind to me,
I value someone who is cuddly,
I value someone who is thoughtful,
This is me.

I like playing with my brother,
I like doing gymnastics,
I like delicious pancakes,
I like baking cake,
I like relaxing in my bed,
This is me.

Mahrosh Fatima (7)
Smith's Wood Primary Academy, Smith's Wood

Outstanding Olly

I have green eyes that are green as leaves,
I have curls that are as curly as noodles,
I have white skin colour,
This is me.
I am as friendly as a bunny,
I am as kind as a teacher,
I am as cool as a footballer,
This is me.
I value someone who is trustworthy and kind,
I trust someone as kind as family,
I need someone who makes me laugh,
This is me.
I like to play football,
I like baking delicious chocolate cake,
I like playing with Lego and Play-Doh,
This is me.

Olly Herbert (8)
Smith's Wood Primary Academy, Smith's Wood

Amazing Ava This Is Me

I have blonde, thick hair,
I have eyes as blue as diamonds,
I have pink shiny glasses,
This is me.

I am a funny, smart girl,
I am as honest as Santa,
I am calm and playful,
This is me.

I value someone who is kind and trustworthy,
I value someone who I can trust,
I value someone who is kind,
This is me.

I like playing with my friends,
I like playing gymnastics and cartwheels,
I like baking cupcakes and cakes,
This is me.

Ava Hill (8)
Smith's Wood Primary Academy, Smith's Wood

Happy Hazel

I have brown, fluffy hair,
I have eyes as dark as chocolate,
I have small, gold earrings,
This is me.

I am funny and beautiful
I am as pretty as a model
I am smart and intelligent
This is me.

I value someone who can make me giggle.
I value someone who I can trust,
I value someone who is friendly,
This is me.

I like flipping in gymnastics,
I like baking in the kitchen,
I like dancing with cool dance moves
This is me.

Hazel Lang-Amug (7)
Smith's Wood Primary Academy, Smith's Wood

Delightful Lilly-Rose

I have long, straight hair,
I have eyes as brown as a magic church.
I have cute, small ears. This is me.

I am as light as a unicorn of gold,
I am smart and intelligent,
I am as encouraging as Florence Nightingale.
This is me.

I value someone who doesn't talk about me behind my back,
I value someone who I think is trustworthy.
This is me.
I like reading.
I like doing magic science.
I like being at a brilliant school.
This is me.

Lilly-Rose Manders (7)
Smith's Wood Primary Academy, Smith's Wood

Jumping Jaiden

I have black, big fluffy hair,
I have mini brown eyes as brown as my skin,
I have tonnes of footballs, lots of different colours,
This is me.

I am a fun and exciting person,
I am a nice, trustworthy guy,
This is me.

I value someone who is nice,
I value someone who listens,
I value someone who plays with me,
This is me.

I like playing FIFA,
I like playing football,
I like playing games,
I like jumping,
This is me.

Jaiden-Epie Nnoko (8)
Smith's Wood Primary Academy, Smith's Wood

This Is Me Spectacular Sophie

I have straight blonde hair
I have eyes as blue as the sky
I have lots of toys
This is me.

I am a cool and funny kid,
I am calm when I do yoga,
I am a smart and interesting girl,
This is me.

I value someone who is thoughtful,
I value someone who is funny,
I value someone who is friendly,
This is me.

I like building Lego,
I like doing arts and crafts,
I like watching movies and seeing my family,
This is me.

Sophie Mullins (8)
Smith's Wood Primary Academy, Smith's Wood

Special Summer

I have short, blonde hair,
I have green eyes like grass,
I have white skin as milk,
This is me.

I am a smart silly girl,
I am unremembered like Miss Cruise.
I am a cool, nice girl,
This is me.

I value someone who I can trust.
I value someone who is responsible,
I value someone who is calm,
This is me.

I like reading books with my sister,
I like chilling with my mum,
I like playing on my Xbox with my sister.

Summer Rose (7)
Smith's Wood Primary Academy, Smith's Wood

Happy Harrison

I have short blonde hair,
I have eyes as blue as the sky,
I have hairy legs,
This is me!

I am smart as a magician,
I am cool as a billionaire,
I am kind,
This is me!

I value someone who is friendly,
I value someone truthful and honest,
I value someone excited,
This is me!

I like to play in goal like Martinez,
I like playing my PS4 and I play FIFA 22,
I like making delicious packed lunch,
This is me.

Harrison Turner (8)
Smith's Wood Primary Academy, Smith's Wood

Epic Ethan

I have fluffy, short hair
I have little legs,
I have strong feet,
This is me.

I am a smart, random boy,
I am as funny as a clown,
I am as intelligent as a spy,
This is me.

I value someone who will play with me,
I value someone that will cheer me up,
I value someone that is sensible,
This is me.

I like eating food,
I like playing with my friends,
I like to play Xbox and blast music
This is me.

Ethan Watkins (7)
Smith's Wood Primary Academy, Smith's Wood

This Is Me I'm Terrific Tayah

I have curly brown hair,
I have eyes as brown as chocolate,
I am eight,
This is me.

I am a crazy girl,
I am as calm as a koala,
I am kind,
This is me.

I value someone that is reliable,
I value someone that will make me smile,
I value someone that will make me laugh,
This is me.

I like going to the skatepark,
I love going rollerblading,
I like relaxing in bed watching YouTube,
This is me.

Tayah Stephens (8)
Smith's Wood Primary Academy, Smith's Wood

This Is Me... Amazing Aarya

I have long, black hair,
I have chocolate eyes as brown as wood.
I have loads of dresses,
This is me.

I am a small, short girl,
I am as funny as a comedian,
I am as hyper as a dog,
This is me.

I value someone who can make me laugh,
I value someone who is chatty,
I value someone who is a bit weird,
This is me.

I like eating cupcakes,
I like playing Roblox,
I like sleeping,
This is me.

Aarya Patel (7)
Smith's Wood Primary Academy, Smith's Wood

This Is Jack This Is Me`

I have long pouffy hair,
I have eyes as blue as the ocean,
I have hairy legs,
This is me.

I am a nice boy,
I am clever and smart,
I am a fanboy,
This is me.

I like reading,
I like swimming,
I like having mango every evening,
I value someone who I can trust,
This is me.

I value someone who I can trust,
I value someone who is friendly,
I value someone who is smart,
This is me.

Jack Phillips (8)
Smith's Wood Primary Academy, Smith's Wood

This Is Me This Is Marvellous Me

I have long blonde hair,
I have blue bright crystal eyes,
I have lots of pretty shiny shelves,
This is me!

I am a clever girl,
I am as smart as a teacher,
I am helpful,
This is me!

I can be friendly all the time,
I can be a good friend to others,
I can be naughty and good all day,
This is me!

I love playing with friends,
I like love playing with my mum,
I love playing and dancing.

Poppy Andrews (7)
Smith's Wood Primary Academy, Smith's Wood

I Am Seanna

I am Seanna and I hope to be the best I can be,
I am violent when I do kickboxing,
I love the people I see around me,
I think about my family all day,
I am aware of my surroundings,
I am not anyone else,
I am myself,
I am strong enough to fight back,
I won't be taken for granted
I am who I want to be,
I am hyper and artistic,
I am myself,
I am Seanna,
And I am proud of who I am.

Seanna Tipper (10)
Smith's Wood Primary Academy, Smith's Wood

Incredible Isabelle

I have long brown hair,
I have brown eyes as brown as chocolate,
This is me.

I am hyper and happy,
I am as smart as a scientist,
I am weird,
I am tall,
This is me.

I value someone who can make me laugh,
I value someone who I can trust,
I value someone who is friendly,
This is me.

I like being with friends and family,
I like drawing,
This is me.

Isabelle Hickin (7)
Smith's Wood Primary Academy, Smith's Wood

Kind Bella

I have long brown hair,
I have eyes brown as mud,
I have been wearing my school uniform,
This is me.

I am cool,
I am weird,
I am cute,
This is me.

I value someone who is funny also kind,
I value someone happy,
I value someone who knows my mind,
This is me.

My hobby is gaming
My hobby is typing
My hobby is making paper planes
This is me.

Isabella Walton (7)
Smith's Wood Primary Academy, Smith's Wood

Fantastic Flynn

I have long dark hair,
I have big legs,
I have thick skin,
This is me.

I am funny,
I am as kind as my ten-year-old dog,
I am cool like ice,
I value someone who is kind,
I value someone who can keep a secret,
I value someone that can make me laugh,
This is me.

I like watching my mum,
I like watching Cruella De Vil,
I like jumping
This is me.

Flynn Hickling (7)
Smith's Wood Primary Academy, Smith's Wood

This Is Me

T eddy is my favourite toy,
H ot dinner is my favourite food at school,
I have friends named Lilly and Milly Mae.
S quishes are my favourite thing to play with.

I like to ride my bike,
S wimming is my favourite thing to do,

M y favourite food is yummy scrummy pizza,
E lephants are my favourite animals.

Autumn Rose (7)
Smith's Wood Primary Academy, Smith's Wood

This Is Me

T he weekend is my favourite
H appy and funny me,
I went on holiday a year ago,
S cary slimy snakes scare me.

I don't like burnt bacon,
S eeking is fun because I like to scare my little sisters.

M y little sisters scare me,
E ven because my eyes are blue and different I still love my family.

Evanna Howell-Roberts (7)
Smith's Wood Primary Academy, Smith's Wood

This Is Me

T oday I rode my scooter to the park,
H as my big sister stolen my toy?
I am an animal lover of cats,
S cootering is my favourite thing to do,

I am sad when my kitten is,
S ometimes I annoy my sister,

M y sister chases me,
E very day I play with Lucy and Lexie.

Millie Duffen (7)
Smith's Wood Primary Academy, Smith's Wood

This Is Me

T aking blaze to the field is great fun.
H appy playing with my friends.
I like to go to school.
S mell of pasta is my favourite.

I like to go to school.
S piders freak me out.

M y friend Callum plays with me.
E very day I try harder.

Riley Summers (7)
Smith's Wood Primary Academy, Smith's Wood

This Is Me

T hankful for everyone who loves me.
H elpful and caring is who I am.
I am independent.
S ometimes I like to swim with my friends.

I am funny.
S ome friends I bond with.

M inecraft is my favourite game.
E yes that look up to the sky.

Bradley Morris (8)
Smith's Wood Primary Academy, Smith's Wood

This Is Me

T oday I went on my bike, and
H olidays are my favourite thing,
I sometimes feel sad,
S o I watch TV

I like maths, it is cool,
S cooting is my favourite thing to do,

M y favourite food is fish and chips,
E ating is healthy.

Kacie-Leigh Snook (7)
Smith's Wood Primary Academy, Smith's Wood

This Is Me

T oday I watched TV,
H air is golden like the sun,
I am very hungry today,
S wings make me smile,

I am eight in July,
S omeday I can go places on my own,

M y favourite show is Sam and Cat,
E very day I play with Chantelle.

Amelia Bunford (7)
Smith's Wood Primary Academy, Smith's Wood

I Am Me

I am Nouria, I am me
I'm a ten-year-old, you see
I'm crazy, weird and really happy.
Sometimes I'm sad and can be lonely
Yet I'm mean and quite angry.
When I am dull, I charge like a bull
So you see, I'm more than the ten-year-old girl.
I am Nouria, I am me.

Nouria Mata (10)
Smith's Wood Primary Academy, Smith's Wood

This Is Me

Everybody loves me
I love ice cream.
I like to watch TikTok.
I am caring and lovely.
I love ice cream with chocolate swirls and sprinkles.
I love going to the zoo because of the tigers.
Sometimes I love making my own.
Minecraft is my favourite game.
My name is Cialan.

Cialan Nolan (7)
Smith's Wood Primary Academy, Smith's Wood

This Is Me

I am seven, that makes me young,
I love my cat, he's really cute,
I can't live without him, he's soft,
He's cute I just want to kiss him,
He has sweet ears that are cute,
Little a bit he's silly that's he's funny,
He looks cute and soft.

Lucy Roberts (7)
Smith's Wood Primary Academy, Smith's Wood

This Is Me

T all, dark brown hair,
H elpful friends to help,
I nteresting in games,
S illy is what I am,

I am good at basketball,
S wimming is the best,

M y favourite food is chocolate,
E yes are dark blue.

Vinny Harper (7)
Smith's Wood Primary Academy, Smith's Wood

The Loving Poem

Loving that's how I can be
I'm helpful and kind to everyone
I'm interesting sometimes
And I love to play basketball
And football and I love the
Game Spider-Man, I love everything
And I like playing tennis
My eyes are light blue.

Louie Simmonds (7)
Smith's Wood Primary Academy, Smith's Wood

This Is Me

R espectful is my thing
I 'm a kind boy
L ike to be a funny person
E yes as blue as the sky
Y ellow bananas are my favourite fruit.

Riley Stanley (8)
Smith's Wood Primary Academy, Smith's Wood

All About Me

I am singing and small
My favourite colour is gold,
My special food is noodles,
Eight is my age,
You Mom are the best
Friendship is my favourite ever.

Finley Andrews (7)
Smith's Wood Primary Academy, Smith's Wood

My Life

My little eyes are watching all you say and do
And when I grow up big and tall
I want to be like you,
I admire to be the person that you are
You're the best friend I could have
You're my bright and shining star.
I look in the mirror
And what do I see?
I see me
No one else can be.
I am precious
I am glad to be me.
My hair, my face
My personality

Beverly Garia (7)
St Stephen's CE Primary School, Westminster

Artistic Me

I am an artist, and I like to draw
I draw pictures which are on my door
I draw and draw, step by step
I never drew pictures while I slept
I first use my brain
To help me get into the game
Then second I give it a hard try
At the end, I hope I will not sigh
When my picture is done, I will give it a look
To me, it is like an illustration of a book.

Sumaya Nur (7)
St Stephen's CE Primary School, Westminster

A Day Horse Riding

One day, I came home from school
I got changed to go horse riding
It was a very windy day
I was on Silver, my favourite horse
In the whole world
It was a group lesson
There were two more people in the lesson
We were doing jumping at the end
All of a sudden, a tornado came
All of the horses hated it and all the riders fell off
But I didn't
Then the tornado came and swept me and Silver
The tornado left and I fell off Silver but we were all okay
That was the end of the day
I got scared that day but in the end
We were all okay and that is the main thing.

Isabel Rhodes (11)
The Kibworth School, Kibworth Beauchamp

Things I Wanted And Would Like To Be

I wanted to be a doctor for a couple of years
I wanted to help people
And learn how the body works
Then I found that you would be tired
And it had sparse perks

I wanted to be a teacher
I wanted to turn children into scientists
Lawyers, vets, the list goes on
Then I found that it wasn't for me
I didn't like reading
And the thought of being a teacher was gone

I wanted to be an astronaut
I wanted to mark flags on the moon
And float in space
But I only wanted to do that job
Because everyone else did
I went on a fake dream chase

I wanted to be a vet
I wanted to help animals
And get forsaken birds out of wooden logs
That was until I grew a fear of dogs

I really, really would've liked to have been a lawyer
And help people find their way to freedom
But I'm not good at persuading people
And it would cause a conundrum

I wanted to be an author
I actually got a book published
This job stuck with me for a long time
But I wrote poems for a while
And it takes me ages to rhyme

Now I want to be an architect
And plan houses for people
I haven't given up on this one
And seems to be working out
I have learnt in order to find something you like
You have to be resilient and patient.

Alaina Scott (11)
The Kibworth School, Kibworth Beauchamp

The Autumn Fall

The falls of leaves flowing to the ground
Looking around, this lovely village is a present itself
The cold crisp air circling around me
All the clouds have disappeared
Making it just like Mount Everest
A damp dull autumn morning was just dawning
As all villagers were making their morning run to the corner shop
Businessmen jumped in their cars with their gloomy wretched faces
As I nearly tripped over because of my laces
Market sellers up early in the morning
Trading their fruit for money
And giving everyone a fair morning

I headed back home and I saw an old friend
"Hello, how are you on this fine morning?"
She said in a jolly voice
I answered back, "I'm excellent, thank you! How about you?"

"I'm good, well I better be going, bye!" she
said happily
I carried on with my day and took my boots off
And let them drain on the path outside my house
All the mud was all over me and my dog
called Sunshine.

Orla Kempster (11)
The Kibworth School, Kibworth Beauchamp

Me

When I'm older, I want to be a builder
Because I like to build stuff as a hobby
I would hate to be in an office all day
Since I am an outdoors person
My favourite animal is a monkey
Since they are almost like humans
And we evolved from them
They are very cute and make me laugh
My friends are great
I have known my best friend almost my whole life
My new friends are amazing
I haven't known them for even a year
But they make me really happy
I have a few other friends from my old primary school
And they are amazing too.

Izzy Moore (11)
The Kibworth School, Kibworth Beauchamp

The Day I Met Ryan Reynolds

One day, I was walking on the street
I was quite happy, I felt complete
Suddenly, across the road
I saw a man who I do not loathe
I ran over to him all excited
Trying to get my mixed feelings united
It was only my favourite man named Ryan
I started to roar like a lion
I began to scream
My emotions together like a team
I asked him for an autograph
After he gave it to me, I began to laugh
I left that day and went to frame the piece
My happiness was finally at peace.

Noah Purves (11)
The Kibworth School, Kibworth Beauchamp

The Life Of Me

I was born five weeks early
On the 2nd of August 2010
I would be in year six
If I had been born on the right date
I've always thought I had a long lost twin
My dream jobs are to be
A director, writer or an actor

Recently, my dad has left
To go on tour, he is a musician
So it's been harder
To get to school on time
In the morning

I'm pretty good at maths
As well as English
I am good at music
It's hard to distinguish.

Ennio Pizzorno (11)
The Kibworth School, Kibworth Beauchamp

Me And My Moon

Me and my moon,
You fly high in the sky,
But when I cry,
You come to comfort me,
Oh, my darling moon,
I love your smile,
Please just stay awhile,
Oh, my darling moon,
I hate it when you cry,
Please don't go,
You don't have to say goodbye,
When you leave,
I feel incomplete,
Oh, my darling moon,
I wish you the best,
Have fun with your stars,
And may I go and rest,
Till next time, my moon,
I wish you the best.

Milli Coulter-Crozier (11)
The Kibworth School, Kibworth Beauchamp

Elliot Hartley

E nthusiastic, electric
L oving, loyal
L aid-back
I maginative, indepedent
O CD, orange
T alented, teachable

H appy, hate loud noises
A ble, accurate
R azzle-dazzle, radiant
T errific, thankful
L egendary, likeable
E xtravagant, eager
Y ippee! Yay!

Elliot Hartley (11)
The Kibworth School, Kibworth Beauchamp

A Schoolgirl

I was walking to school and I saw a cat
The cat walked up to me
I took a second and stared at it
When I got to school, a message went around
That there was a missing cat
I saw a picture, it was a mixture of black and white
I was walking home and saw it dead in the middle of the road.

Sophie Boulter (11)
The Kibworth School, Kibworth Beauchamp

Be You

You may be autistic
But you still need to be optimistic
Even if you have a frown
You still need to carry your crown

If you like yellow or blue
Everyone believes in you
Never give up hope
And never say nope!

Imogen (11)
The Kibworth School, Kibworth Beauchamp

All About Me!

My name is Charlie
Things I like are
Footie, cooking, having best mates
Chilling out in the lounge, playing with my puppy
My puppy is one year old and he is naughty
He had a hard time with his old owner so
we got him.

Charlie Robinson (12)
The Kibworth School, Kibworth Beauchamp

The Eralp Flavour: The Gamer

A wonderful gamer
I move as fast as the buttons I press on
the controller
Give me chocolate and I'll go hyper
And then after that, start to shoot my sniper
As I play Call of Duty, I can't control the controller

I am a startling mathematician
Ones and zeros run through my head
The same as I do outside with my friends
Words don't matter much, as I prefer
numbers instead

I use my love for numbers more than words
To become the next billionaire gamer technician
I run outside pretending to be a video
game character
Helping me to blow away the competition

I can see myself slashing a horde of zombies
That's why they call me the Zombie Exterminator

I am sitting with a sniper in hand
Call me for duty, get set, I'm ready
Watch out! I'll be back, I'll be the next Terminator

I'll be thrashing, smashing, and slashing
Through the blood and guts
This is me!
The next billionaire gamer
Adding a pinch of Eralp flavour.

Tahir Eralp Guzel (11)
The Literacy House International, Tintagel

Hide And Tickle Seek

Sometimes we play a game
It's called 'hide and tickle seek'
It's my favourite game to play
With her, it brings me lots of laughter
When I play the game
It makes me have enjoyment
Inside my heart
Whenever I play the game.

Theo Oryem (7)
Thorpedene Primary School, Shoeburyness

Young Writers

YOUNG WRITERS INFORMATION

We hope you have enjoyed reading this book – and that you will continue to in the coming years.

If you're the parent or family member of an enthusiastic poet or story writer, do visit our website www.youngwriters.co.uk/subscribe and sign up to receive news, competitions, writing challenges and tips, activities and much, much more! There's lots to keep budding writers motivated!

If you would like to order further copies of this book, or any of our other titles, then please give us a call or order via your online account.

Young Writers
Remus House
Coltsfoot Drive
Peterborough
PE2 9BF
(01733) 890066
info@youngwriters.co.uk

Join in the conversation!
Tips, news, giveaways and much more!

YoungWritersUK   YoungWritersCW   youngwriterscw